Dragons & Monsters

The parable of the two sons

Chris Hudson

Acknowledgments

We would like to thank Wylva Davies and Val Bulman for their help. We would also like to express our gratitude to the following schools for trialling the material.

St Mark's C of E, Worsley, Manchester
Parkview Primary, Oakwood, Derby
St Andrew's Primary, Salisbury
Holy Trinity Primary, Bradley Stoke, Bristol

The Stapleford Centre is an interdenominational centre which aims to produce materials, and offer in-service courses, to resource the teaching of Christianity in schools. Full details of courses and publications are available from:

The Stapleford Centre
The Old Lace Mill
Frederick Road
Stapleford
Nottingham
NG9 8FN
Tel: 0115 939 6270
Fax: 0115 939 2076
E-mail: admin@stapleford-centre.org
Website: www.stapleford-centre.org

Published by
The Bible Reading Fellowship
First Floor, Elsfield Hall
15–17 Elsfield Way, Oxford OX2 8FG
ISBN 1 84101 206 8
First published 2001
10 9 8 7 6 5 4 3 2 1 0

Acknowledgments
Unless otherwise stated, scripture quotations are taken from the Good News Bible published by The Bible Societies/HarperCollins Publishers Ltd, UK © American Bible Society 1966, 1971, 1976, 1992, used with permission.

A catalogue record for this book is available from the British Library

Printed and bound in Malta

Contents

How to use this book

This book provides the following:

- ★ Masters for a Big Book
- ★ Activities for literacy work (word, sentence and text level)
- ★ RE follow-up ideas
- ★ RE activity sheets/stimulus material
- ★ Differentiated RE activities
- ★ Ideas for reflection/learning from religion

Parables

Parables are stories with a spiritual/moral meaning. They are an example of non-literal language, along with metaphors and similes.

RE and literacy work

As well as the Big Book masters, this book contains a bank of activities at word, sentence and text level; literacy activity sheets; RE follow-up and RE activity sheets. There is some information for teachers on some of the activity sheets; this can be removed using office 'white-out' before copying. The material in this book can be used in RE and literacy time but the focus will be different in literacy and RE. Literacy teaching should not replace RE; neither should RE replace literacy teaching.

The Big Book

The story can be used in RE or literacy time. The masters for the Big Book can be used in a number of ways:

- ★ Photocopied on to acetates
- ★ Enlarged and photocopied to create a Big Book
- ★ Photocopied to create small pupil books

The pictures can be coloured either by hand or by scanning into the computer and using a paint programme on parts of the drawings. (Some software can do this.)

Suggested activities

- ★ Use items in the text to tell the story.
- ★ Pupils can mime or role-play situations in the story.
- ★ Ask questions about possible consequences of actions and what might happen next.
- ★ Bring out any moral issues for discussion: 'Do you think Jack was right to…?'
- ★ Ask pupils to read sections with appropriate expression.
- ★ Ask their opinion about what is happening in the story.
- ★ Relate the issues in the stories to pupils' experiences.

QCA links (England)

Parables link to the following units in the QCA RE schemes: 1D, 2B, 3C, 3D, 5C, 5D, 6C and 6F.

Handling biblical material

Pupils should be told where the story comes from and why it is important to Christians. Christian material should be introduced: 'Today we are looking at a story from the Bible (or based on a story from the Bible) which is important to Christians.' This allows pupils to identify with the story or to study it from another perspective.

Dragons and monsters

'Billy! Jack! Where are you? It's time to tidy up your rooms!'

Billy and Jack were playing at the bottom of the garden.

They had been making a very interesting castle out of bits of old cardboard boxes and some planks of wood. There was a drawbridge, a secret door, and slits for shooting arrows in case any dangerous fire-breathing dragons came charging down the garden path.

Something dangerous did come down the path. It wasn't a dragon, but something much worse. It was Mum! She was not happy!

'Billy! Jack! I told you ten minutes ago to come in! I've been upstairs, and your rooms are a tip! Now, I'm going to start cooking the lunch. You've got half an hour to sort out your rooms before we eat. After that, we can go down to the park – but only if your rooms are tidy. Do you understand?' The boys nodded sadly, but Jack was cross, even though he did want to go to the park later.

'Why have we got to stop now? We were enjoying ourselves!'

Mum gave him a long stare, then spoke quietly.

'Half an hour – do you understand?'

They nodded again, so she turned, and disappeared back along the path. A dragon would have been much more welcome than this.

With a sigh, it was Billy who climbed out of the castle. Jack stayed put. He thought Mum was mean. What do you think?

'Come on then!' said Billy. Jack didn't move. 'Aren't you coming?' Jack shook his head. Billy was curious. 'Why?'

'It's not fair! I was enjoying myself.'

'Well, I'm going anyway!' Billy ran up the path. He wanted to go to the park as well, and knew that Mum always meant exactly what she said.

Jack sat and sulked in his castle. Everything was quiet. There was nobody to share his clever ideas with. He had wanted to make some clever secret weapon that would squirt dragons with water, but it wasn't as much fun now. The game was over. It was so unfair! Why did it have to be like this?

Meanwhile, Billy was up in his room. It was very untidy, but he had found a very interesting electronic game under his bed, so he sat down to play it for five minutes. After all, there would be plenty of time, wouldn't there?

'Oh rats!' Jack climbed out of the castle, and walked up the path towards the house. He thought he'd better get on with tidying his room before he got into trouble.

Meanwhile, back in his bedroom, Billy was still playing the game. He was now on another level. 'Just another five minutes,' he said to himself. His bedroom wasn't getting any tidier.

Jack was now in his own bedroom, picking up clothes and putting things back in boxes. He imagined he was driving an army of monsters back into their caves, pushing them back and saving the world. Jack wasn't going to let them mess up his bedroom! He'd show them! He took out his special secret weapon (the waste bin) and cleared up all the rubbish that littered his floor.

Billy was now on the next level in his electronic game. He was feeling pleased with himself, but his room hadn't changed.

'There! I've finished!' Jack looked at his tidy room. The monsters were nowhere to be seen, and everything was in its right place. He'd won!

'Lunchtime!' Mum called up the stairs. The two boys came down. Jack had a smile on his face, but Billy looked a bit worried. He knew that after lunch, Mum would want to see his room. What would she say?

How to not tidy your bedroom

1. Pick up everything on the floor and put it on the bed.
2. Now pick up everything on the bed, and put it back on the floor.
3. Open some drawers and shove some things in. Don't forget to mix up bits of different games and toys.
4. Hide any dirty washing under the bed. Don't forget to lose one of each pair of socks.
5. Move a few things on shelves from here to there and from there to here. (Don't bother doing any dusting – there'll just be more dust by next week.)
6. Don't forget to play with something as you do all this. It shows that you're not thinking about what you are doing.
7. After a few minutes of this, shout, 'I've finished!' and then hope that nobody comes to look. Don't forget to hide if they do.

Two kinds of people

You find two kinds of people,
Those who do and those who don't;
Some say they want to do it,
But after that they won't.
But if you look behind the words,
The fussing and the chatter;
It's not the words that count the most,
It's what we do that matters.

Top ten children's excuses for not tidying their bedrooms

Count up from number 10.

1. It is tidy, I've already done it.
2. I can't find the waste bin.
3. Somebody else must have come in and messed it up.
4. I did it last week.
5. I've got to go to school now.
6. I've got to go to bed now.
7. My favourite TV programme is just about to start.
8. Nobody else has to do it. It's not fair.
9. It's supposed to be like that – we're playing a game.
10. I'll do it tomorrow.

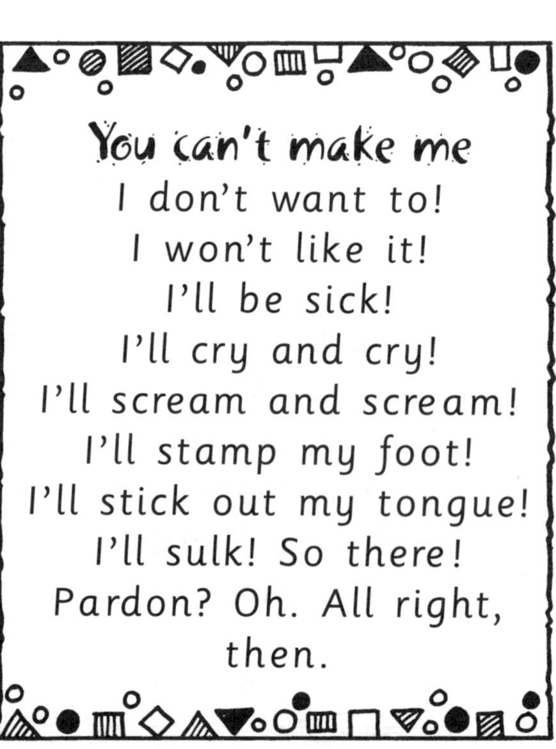

You can't make me

I don't want to!
I won't like it!
I'll be sick!
I'll cry and cry!
I'll scream and scream!
I'll stamp my foot!
I'll stick out my tongue!
I'll sulk! So there!
Pardon? Oh. All right,
then.

Parables

A parable is a short story with a message. Jesus wanted his ideas to be remembered by lots of people, so he used parables to explain things. Parables are everyday stories. Jesus would talk about things that were familiar to his audience. He would talk about what it was like to make bread, or what it was like to lose something and then find it. Each parable had its own deeper message.

Here are the two sons from one of Jesus' parables. Invent names for them. Turn over to hear Jesus' story about them.

The parable of the two sons

Matthew 21:28–32

Jesus was teaching people about how they could live their lives in a way that pleased God, but some of them didn't agree with him.

'God loves us anyway,' they said. 'We are very good people!'

'There's more to it than that,' replied Jesus.

‘Listen – there was once a man who had two sons. He went to the eldest one and said, “Son, please go and work in our vineyard today.”

‘“I don’t want to,” the lad answered. But later he changed his mind and went.

‘The father then went to the younger son and asked him to do the same thing.

‘“Of course I’ll go!” said the boy. But he didn’t.

'So then,' Jesus asked the crowd, 'which one of the two did as his father wanted?'

'The eldest,' they answered.

'Exactly. There are some people who are sorry for what they have done and want to change. They hear God's message and they act on it. They are like the first son in the story. Some people are like the second son. They are people who have heard God's message but do nothing!'

Jesus didn't make many friends on that day!

Activity Bank

Word level

Year 2

TERM 1

(W8) Use a page of text to teach understanding of 'vowel' and 'consonant'.

(W1, W2, W3) Look for examples of vowel phonemes (park, garden, charging) and long vowel phonemes (shooting, rooms) in the text.

TERM 2

(W4) Discuss the use of compound words in the text, splitting them into their component parts: cardboard, drawbridge. See Worksheet B.

(W5) Pick out examples of syllables in multi-syllabic words: dra-gon, int-er-est-ing, dang-er-ous. Use this to help with learning new spellings.

(W8) Look for words with common negative prefixes: untidy, disappeared.

TERM 3

(W2) Reinforce Term 2 (W5) work.

(W6) Investigate words which have the same spelling patterns, but different sounds: though/thought, weapon/meant/mean.

(W10) Collect and discuss synonyms and other alternative words/phrases for those in the text: disappeared, interesting, tidy, are a tip.

Sentence level

Year 2

TERM 1

(S2) Find examples of words and phrases that link sentences: after, then, meanwhile.

(S3) Study the use of capital letters, full stops, commas and exclamation marks. How would the flow of the sentences and the story be affected if they were removed or replaced with something else? See Worksheet C.

(S5) Study the use of capitals in names and titles.

TERM 2

(S4) Look for examples of grammatical agreement: it was, we were, your rooms are.

(S5) Study the use of tense in the first five paragraphs of the story, noting the use of the past tense for narration and the present tense for dialogue—although Mum's second speech uses past, present and future tense. Can you spot where?

(S6) Identify the use of speech marks. Point out that publishers usually use single inverted commas for speech, while many schools continue to teach the use of double inverted commas for writing. Look for other examples in books. See Worksheet C.

Use Term 1 (S2) activity for consolidation.

TERM 3

(S1) Together, read parts of the text aloud with appropriate expression and intonation, showing due regard for grammar and punctuation.

(S3) Look at the use of standard forms of verbs, and how changing their tense would change the sense or meaning (came, told, are). See also note for Term 2 (S5).

(S7) Compare the different types of question in the text: who is addressing whom?

Use Term 1 (S2) activity for consolidation.

Text level

Year 2

TERM 1

Class: (T5) Share and discuss the main points of the story. What were the reasons that Mum gave for tidying the rooms? What reasons did the boys have—and why do you think things turned out the way they did?

(T6) Discuss: what makes the grown-ups who look after you cross?

Group: (T4) Create simple story maps/cartoon strips that list/illustrate the main events of the story in numerical order. For simplicity, emphasize use of 'stick men' and speech bubbles. (Fold an A4 sheet into six to provide six frames.) Allow two sessions for this.

▶

(T4) Use Worksheet D to discuss the significance of the story's title and order of events.
(T5, T10) Write imaginary letters of apology from the boys to Mum about the untidy rooms.
Plenary: Share these examples. What did we all think were the main events of the story? What do we think could happen next? What alternative endings could there be?

TERM 2
Class: (T6) What words would you use to describe each of the characters in the story? How do you think they would talk to each other in a situation—for example, the initial garden scene?
(T4, T5) What do you think the boys would have been saying to each other before Mum appeared? (Emphasize the fantasy aspect of their game.)
Group: (T7) Plan together a short dramatic reading of the opening scene. Divide the children into threes, so that they each have a role. Use the actual dialogue as a basis, but also add some more lines. These can be improvised or scripted.
Plenary: Share some of the group readings. Discuss what the conversation would have gone like after Mum discovered the untidy bedroom. What would the consequences have been then? What do you think the boys would have been saying to each other?

TERM 3
Class: (T4, T7) Explain that this story is based on an oral parable told by Jesus. (It was written down many years after he told it.) Read both, compare the two and discuss any common themes and obvious differences. What do you think is the parable's message? Use Worksheet A, which contains the original Bible story.
Group: (T10) Write your own version of the parable, using two different characters in a different situation: for example, cleaning out a pet's cage, going to the shops.
Plenary: Share some of the stories. Have they kept the common thread of the parable?

Literacy Worksheet A

The parable of the two sons

'Listen – there was once a man who had two sons. He went to the eldest one and said, "Son, please go and work in our vineyard today."

"I don't want to," the lad answered. But later, he changed his mind and went. The father then went to the younger son and asked him to do the same thing.

"Of course I'll go!" said the boy. But he didn't.'

'So then,' Jesus asked the crowd, 'which one of the two did as his father wanted?'

'The eldest,' they answered.

Activity 1

'Dragons and monsters' is based on this parable by Jesus. The author has taken the story told by Jesus, and then placed it in a different setting. Read/listen to both stories, and then use the table to say what is similar and what is different.

Similar	Different

What is the message of both stories?

Activity 2

Draw and label one event from 'Dragons and Monsters' which isn't in the parable told by Jesus.

Literacy Worksheet B

Activity 1

'Compound words' are made out of other words that have been stuck together. Can you pull these compound words apart in the right place to find the other words?

drawbridge	=	draw	+	bridge
cardboard	=		+	
bedroom	=		+	
everything	=		+	
lunchtime	=		+	

Can you think of any more words that do this? Look round your classroom and see if you can spot any things whose names are compound words. List them here.

Activity 2

Can you work out the compound word that goes with each drawing? If you can, then make some more!

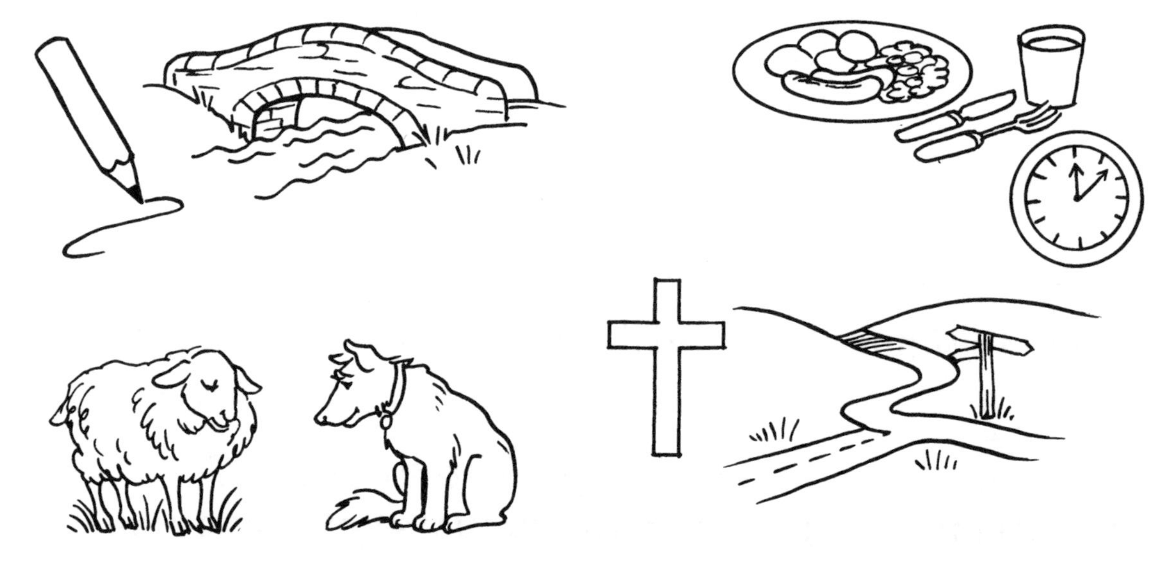

Literacy Worksheet C

Activity 1

All the capitals, full stops, commas and exclamation marks have been lost in this passage. Can you put them back in, so that it makes sense?

billy and jack were playing at the bottom of the garden they had been making a very interesting castle out of bits of old cardboard boxes and some planks of wood there was a drawbridge a secret door and slits for shooting arrows in case any dangerous fire-breathing dragons came charging down the garden path something dangerous did come down the path it wasn't a dragon but something much worse it was mum

Activity 2

Do the same with this passage.

a) add full stops
b) add capitals
c) add commas
d) add exclamation marks
e) add question marks
f) add speech marks

billy jack i told you ten minutes ago to come in your rooms are a tip jack was cross why have we got to stop now we were enjoying ourselves mum gave him a good stare half an hour—do you understand she turned then disappeared back up the path come on then said billy jack didn't move it's not fair i was enjoying myself

Literacy Worksheet D

Activity 1

This story is called 'Dragons and Monsters'. Which of these sentences from the story fits best with that title? Choose one, copy it out, illustrate it, and explain why you think it fits with the title.

Activity 2

These sections of story have been numbered and set out in the wrong order. In pairs, cut out and sort them so that they make sense. Then sum up the message of the story in one sentence.

1. Jack sat and sulked in his castle.
2. Billy found a very interesting electronic game under his bed.
3. Jack imagined he was driving an army of monsters back into their caves.
4. 'Lunchtime!' Mum called up the stairs.
5. Jack climbed out of the castle, and walked up the path towards the house.
6. Mum came and told them to tidy their bedrooms.
7. The two boys came downstairs.
8. Billy and Jack had been making a very interesting castle out of bits of old cardboard boxes and some planks of wood.

RE Teacher's Page

The story 'Dragons and monsters' is based on the parable of the two sons (Matthew 21:28–32).

Story framework

(For use with 'Dragons and monsters'.) Jesus liked to teach using stories called parables. This is a version of one of them.

(For use with the actual parable.) The parable of the two sons took place when Jesus was teaching in the Temple, surrounded by religious leaders. They were very critical of the way he welcomed everyone, especially the people they called 'sinners'.

Background material

This story works at two levels. At its most basic, it contrasts the relative worth of words and actions – but in context, it is part of a much bigger idea. Jesus was illustrating two contrasting ideas of spirituality. He spoke with great anger about the proud, legalistic religious attitudes of his time that neglected justice and mercy, but he also acted with great gentleness towards those who realized they'd made a mess of their lives, and wanted to repent, making a fresh start with God.

The two sons symbolize the two attitudes. One son appears to be disobedient, but then meets his father's request. The other is apparently obedient, but only in words. Jesus is contrasting the relative worth of words and actions when it comes to dealing with God. Words are all very well, but useless if they are not backed up with actions.

Conversation starters

- ★ What do you think Mum said when she went to look at their rooms?
- ★ What do you think happened after that?
- ★ How would the boys be feeling at the end of all this?

Religious Education

RE activities

Worksheets E, F and G can be used either to stimulate discussion or in their own right.

BASIC

Listen to the original story (see 'Standard' section, following), verbally answer the questions provided on Worksheet E, and then sum up the message of the story in ten words or less.

STANDARD

Read the parable of the two sons (pages 20–22, Worksheet A, or a child-friendly version of Matthew 21:28–32). Create two labels. Write 'Action' on one and 'Words' on the other. Turn the labels over and put a high price on one and a low price on the other. Think carefully about the parable before you do this. Which did Jesus say was worth more? Why?

EXTENSION

As above, but research and discuss the meaning of the word 'parable' for a dictionary entry. Why do you think Jesus taught people using parables? Research other parables such as the two house-builders (Matthew 7:24–27), the hidden treasure (Matthew 13:44), the pearl (Matthew 13:45), and the sower (Matthew 13:3–9). Children will either need help finding these in a children's Bible, or they should have child-friendly versions prepared.

Reflection/Learning from religion

Read the poem 'Two kinds of people'. Ask, 'Can you think of times when you have said you would do something – and haven't done it? What effect did that have? How could you make it different in future?'

RE Worksheet E

Activity 1

If somebody asks me to do something

I can ______________________________

or I can ______________________________

or I can ______________________________

Activity 2

In his parable, Jesus talked about a father and two sons. He asked them to go and do some work. What happened?

The first son ______________________________

____

The second son ______________________________

____

Which one did Jesus say was better in the end?

____

Why do you think that was? ______________________________

____

____

Activity 3

At the end of the day, what do you think the father would say to his sons?

RE Worksheet F

Activity 1

Read these proverbs. What do you think they mean?

'Actions speak louder than words.'

'Talking is cheap.'

'An empty barrel makes the most noise.'

Activity 2

Do any of them relate to the parable of the two sons? Explain how.

____

____

____

____

____

Activity 3

Do you think the first proverb is good advice? Give a reason.

____

____

____

____

RE Worksheet 6

The story of the two sons is a parable, which is a short story with a message. Jesus used lots of parables to explain things. He would talk about everyday things that were familiar to his audience. He would talk about what it was like to make bread, or what it was like to lose something and then find it. Each parable had its own deeper message.

Activity 1

Write the meaning of the word 'parable' for a short dictionary entry. Why do you think Jesus liked to teach people by using parables?

____

____

____

Activity 2

Find the names of some other parables of Jesus and write their titles here.

____

____

____

Activity 3

Read one parable and re-tell it here in your own words. Use the back of this sheet if you need more space.

____

____

____